"By turns drifting and twitchy, the fragments that comprise MacEachern's evocative, invigorating first book lodge under the skin. Like splinters, or shards of brightly coloured glass, or bones that were always there but you didn't recognize them until now. Sometimes they're broken (sometimes we're broken), sometimes they make something whole."

— STEPHANIE BOLSTER

"Jessi MacEachern's first book of poetry strikes almost as a journal of the pronounced interiority all of us are living these days. A construction of sequences in which each passage on its own is a feast and lark, its poems unfold small mysteries that are dangerously calm, exploring intimate relations lived by women in the space of the house. In the rhythmic arborescence of precise lyric images, there are no totalities. Self-examining but never self-absorbed, MacEachern's poems are saucy and savvy; via a female gaze onto gender and spacings, they pulse with uneasy but hard-won life."

— ERÍN MOURE

"In Jessi MacEachern's spellbinding (and spellblinding) debut, poems glint like slivers of glass but have the force of shrapnel. Shards of text, taut with significance, are read as if we are loosed in dream. MacEachern's language recalls what Nicole Brossard says of "the re-invented language," in which there is "a space for the existence of the woman subject and her desire... space for her singularity as well as her plurality." As one speaker puts it, "our hearts / Nose a line of light in the dust," searching for meaning in a place only few have inhabited. MacEachern bends the light of words and shines directly into the Brossardian "espace inédit," arresting the reader in language's new, peculiar rays."

— GILLIAN SZE

A
NUMBER
OF
STUNNING
ATTACKS

A NUMBER OF NUMBER OF STUNNING ATTACKS

JESSI MACEACHERN

Invisible Publishing
Halifax & Prince Edward County

Library and Archives Canada Cataloguing in Publication

Title: A number of stunning attacks / Jessi MacEachern.

Names: MacEachern, Jessi, 1988- author.

Identifiers: Canadiana (print) 20200393758 | Canadiana (ebook) 20200393774 | ISBN 9781988784656 (softcover) | ISBN 9781988784755 (HTML)

Subjects: LCGFT: Poetry.

Classification: LCC PS8625.E23 N86 2021 | DDC C811/.6—dc23

Edited by Jenny Sampirisi

Cover and interior design by Megan Fildes

With thanks to type designer Rod McDonald

Invisible Publishing is committed to protecting our natural environment. As part of our efforts, both the cover and interior of this book are printed on acid-free 100% post-consumer recycled fibres.

Printed and bound in Canada

Invisible Publishing | Halifax & Prince Edward County
www.invisiblepublishing.com

We acknowledge for their financial support of our publishing program the Canada Council for the Arts, the Ontario Arts Council, and the Government of Canada.

THE MOAT AROUND HER HOME

She keeps a notebook labelled *dreams to have* in which

She is careless in the sunshine

She flirts with car doors
the city is quick

If quickness is a synonym for wit
she has arranged a parade

It is proper that the women should remain indoors
See:

Some creature has gotten in
the sauce   cremini

Blackened garlic   her carpet
a feast for the ceiling eyes

Male bodies flush
                    with squealing

Unclean lives
are best suited to indoor rain

Best considered against a wall against
which the only mirror

Has fallen

Tattered remnants   paper-made fixtures
an altar for the grasshopper carcass

                                              fine

Scribbled contact promises
instant acquaintances

The women are learning

                                    concrete stains

handwritten alterations

A white splinter in her gum

She grins   she wallows
where fallen leaves   are falling still

Who brought the outside in?

She keeps a notebook labelled *dreams to have* in which

The sunset is bound up like a cookbook

Piling its shifting bricks   to low clouds
                    a child surprised

The walls of the home have been a trick of light

Permanent lake   rainwater

Rapid wings   behind
                    Dream's   unhinged door

The difference is quality

A white squirrel has its neck broken by a child
the women are up to their elbows
                                        drowning rabbits
                    in the porcelain sink

One building has too few windows
to accept a sky-born drumbeat

Bridal dresses chlorinate the night

In response to the muted veil

Who provided the corner light?

One piss-yellow beam

the strange man

's open-mouthed laugh

The exciting new organisms we will grow!

Dream is a manicurist
her blackened toes pass the time

She has the necessary people

                                          the necessary persona

to cultivate an underside

Counsel is encouraged

Velvet dallies   against one low stoop
body assumed   phantasm for the ground

The overpass once looked up from the white the insipid

                                        Mildness
the promise in its salamander eyes

An algae continent   attempts to snare
the high-rise building

The liquid respite is not the city's
                                to recount

A longing for whitened coffee

                                   elbows to close

the gap between something or nothing

The women go into the night
running ceramic shards

                          cotton swabs

Yes, at least the maggots are happy!

To wait   arrange
black matter   ebb its passing

This hair consciousness   living drainage
the response   stone-red candies

One large mouth in her pretty face
has learned   others are frigid

Dream remains inside

This is the crime scene

Head of a man
                              split
base of street lamp

Elusive cherubs
                              frolicking
hilly pink remains

                              Dream's sphere
              approaches slowly

Inside men no longer
                              hush refusal
She is thought

to be capable of finding a new way

Bringing bleached handkerchief
to nose plush maggots in cotton folds

Lick any collarbone

The dividing wall will not dissolve
iron
                        will not bend

Her white light's will to please

STAGGER AND SING

His apology is as thick as the sofa cushions
A water glass falls the mattress tips

His shaven head is beneath the bed sheets
The speaker shrieks a light bulb sputters

They are not naked but perfect

Her fat little fingers impede the excuse
In the window they become glass

Dynamite shards glinting elbows lock
Forearms in protestation a cross a fight

Eventual moonlight collides with the wall

In the window their clicking joints keep time
They place their fingers deep inside

The shadow's lilac crown askew
They always seem to be someone

Their lips your lips too our moving
We lay down the avenue exhibitionist

Your lips are trout that swam inside
Her palms a golden watch face

You graze concrete with your spread hands
Spend sunlight with large-headed males

Unspooled time combing the ground
Dailiness vanishing in the crush

He always tries again less a liar
Those sounds so less alone than we are

Duvet is continental drift on the floor below

Ankles kissed by blonder locks than these
Crenulated bodies fold and swerve

In the space cultivated between
She and her so many cherry blossoms

At bloom our hearts
Nose a line of light in the dust

She thinks of you as the surrounding blue

Sky delight of a pastoral poem
In the street-facing window

He thinks he is thinking
Thinking of you

A fixture in the sunlit descent
You're prettier on the outside

She closes the lingering space below his chins
In the morning's hands between their humid bodies

She knocks his teeth against your rising your falling
He keeps your face between her legs

His tongue finds shape to you
Turning peak

You really must
Accidentally her scalp crowns

Nestling her long nose in his throat a siren wails
A dancing breath before courage

Voluptuous layers of man powdered sugar
Placated open nerves

She knew him
Kissed him

Was threatened by
You knew him

Kissed him
Placed your trust in

Yours is the dull voice of a friend
No rising panic no sudden slickness

Stagger and sing of the crucified son
Boy of a bursting mother

A vision of roses

He meant to continue

He set his teeth into the illumination bit
You crawled to his mother's pantry

In her lonely room honeyed breast nipped by the slat blinds
Velvet lipstick lines the demarcation

limbs
air

In the window we are glass fixtures
We are in shards

Quivering jelly suffocates the eggshell wall
We draw thick red tears on the rounded ass

limbs
air

Needle pricks are solid drops
All is slick with love or mimicry

NOTES ON MOVING

She dreams a little in the dark
the city as it no longer exists

& it grew quiet

She wears an armoured breastplate
to greet the fountain's city square

Veil slipping to demonstrate the effect
closing time & space

Her nature is improvisational in approach
she begins with a friendly & relaxed tone

"Love is the difficult realization..."

His letters arrived without consistency

In the studio apartment
her ink-splattered palm

Gently tied in looping calculations & fragrant
yellow spatula leavings

His taut forearm flesh warmed the cool of her hand
his invisible body tormented the dismayed afternoon

It all weighs so heavily

Our feminine organs discerned it
fireflies beat from the knot of his tie

A spiral of lightning-quick whispers flamed
the cheeks of the hushed boy-child

Like a knife he stood in memory
an unshaven lip the transformative flash

We grew quiet

Her body spreads indefinitely beneath the belt
her lacquered white coat askew

She must look to move or be moved
the senses know that absence blots people out

That solace which two different notes
one high one low strike together

Two figures bent as one with vanity of breathing
if we could steal their breath the room would bloom

What angers her is the interruption
of self in drawing up drawing in

Saying to the other, "Yes, dear, I am here."
sequentially touching each other

& then at distance from each other
inevitably she would become

The focus of the print engorged in his lap
dinosaur spine rising with regular indignation

"Do they not see I am here?"

Her heavy bosom deflates two dry-cleaning bags against
a Puritan quilt he puckered his lips

The pungent silence like lice in the gleaming
divine beneath her feathers

& it grew quiet

Without her human limbs she was unable to carry
something other than herself

Is real
the day is like his straying

It grew quiet in the unconscious
without human lungs she discovers vocabulary

& grammar is something the senses know
people blot absence out

Something other than velour
is needed for the day
its purification

He yawned open
the fatal letter
the senses know

The intrinsic connection between digits
grimace exhausted from the room's bodies

Finely ground down to minimal
flesh & barely there bone

Bulging with anticipation he came
it grew quiet in the meeting place

Trouser pockets his fingers tore into
her sealed envelopes

Across the room in the fertile darkness of unconscious
she would shout

We must look to move
the rest is silence
—

How it came to this
his coming against
a tree stump

For our feminine organs

there will be no meaningful study
the heart may think it knows better

& grow quiet

For our visible Dream

in the fertile darkness of grammar
we will destroy

the unconscious

She swerves into orgy of summer
a parishioner kneeling

She leaves her garments
a rhinestone in the parted fabric

If she complains loudly
we must look to be moved

Our soft organs know no distinction
he bought pickled figs he never wrote back

The house licks its teeth clean
threatens the single cluster

Wild flowers abandoned
to streams of vermouth or bleach

The senses know this absence

Elsewhere she ceased
to be isolated & recorded

She returned to the story of wife
one hand shaking salt & bubbling yolk

Inaudible sigh wets the elbow snap
for years she moved among us

& grew quietly in the dark
in the fertile unconscious of those before her

A MINIATURE GENDER

Gender is a good friend

A hurt self on wooden surface
An immediate forgetting

A decaying kaleidoscope
Encouraging the smoke

I've forgotten about morning,

Benjamin attests there can be nothing more pleasant
Than to lie on a sofa and read

Benjamin is something remote from us

Benjamin talks in sun
The city was only ever wrong

Several young people follow

       I,

       I,

       I begin again,

"Amphetamine," he says, "you lose your mind—"
Fully clothed in bed he obsesses over K

To write about a miniature gender
No he in history could stand she

A mirror in the palms of his offering
His offering (anyway) is

                        "Eat a lot of grapefruit."

Gender keeps their several eyes on allwomen

To write about a miniature gender
Inscribe their names on soft flesh

                    Walter
                    K (who does not appear)
                    Andy
                    Bob
                    Frank
                    She (who might be Dream)

Just as the cavalry went
A queen among her sycophants

Carrying the weight of unread books
Hushed perception curdles
                              Movement
Leaves mechanics spins being behind

The automaton plays a winning game
"The art of storytelling—coming to an end," it says

There is a Polaroid of Dylan Warhol cannot see
He says (anyway) "Yeah, well, you should write about girls."

"—"

And? How was it?

Moonshine made the homemade girl say
"Well, it's so great you've had a baby."

I wonder what she will be next,

Gender has all this on video

"He's a has-been,"
Says the thick answering voice of a woman

Who fell in love with
                              His *Collected Kafka*
The ability to tell a tale properly

"Well, he didn't call me up—"   She cannot find a light
Always repeating herself   "You didn't call."

The line has calcified
                              "Maybe you've lost it."

In the dream there are many methods of drawing

Foolscap pencil shavings hollowed prayers. Some world shifts
(just a mouth moving on hopeful reflex) and dissolves

The automaton locks a door. The subjects are left with Kafka
An intelligent meaning to a word

"I was at a cowboy party—" As though this is an excuse for taste

In the everywhere else rub of red
Can she

Hang in there little engine,

You lose our mind. We lose your mind
The figure here is giraffes

Days and pages later
"Grapefruit."

We don't know how to respond to that

A miniature gender

Careens a nook with limbs not their own
Reads one neat paper. Rotates the pencilled lines

A dog in mid bark

Dylan is out of sight. Dylan is presumed lost
Please check your closet

The summer months belong to Gender alone

In the living moss of the untended bedroom
the *Collected Kafka* breeds glow-worms

"You didn't call me up—"   A stutter into hem-haw
"It's been a week and a day."

                    Last glass of red,

Lovely

Mostly

Behind the discarded ideas
A time-worn facial cue

Surprising no one
has left,

She is always repeating herself and Warhol is always saying,

"Groovy."

In love
She does not love

The thick female yes. No one takes up his game
Decides this is all wrong: "It's been eight days."

The hand is always saying, "Must I apologize?"
To higher standards

No one sings,

How sad

It is
Perfect

Fleshless and casting green
No one nods slowly

"Well, what's your name?"
And that is the end of the conversation

The whole thing can stand upright on two legs
The whole thing looks senseless enough

But when it becomes indignant
Has the same sticking sense of a mother

Wading in her
Healing springs
Knowing her

Benjamin asks, "Are you yourself?"

    Yes

    and again
    the answer

    no,

We've learned to want more
To give

Forgetting how to be
We went to nine butcher shops

Bookshops

I think I might be

After all

A NUMBER OF
STUNNING ATTACKS

A woman in acts of sex failed attempt to squeeze the world out
to have a human body   she visits her father

Alcoholism is charming in suburbs where everyone has enough
money to keep   off-balance

When the doorbell rings   A woman does not answer
unless for fresh-cut diamonds   or hay bales

"Your mother was altogether too good for me."

This need to be two in sunlight   mourning greater intimacy
a stranger flushed by her surprise becomes small and able

As two she straightens the mouth's curve

A wheel is a skittish hand   separate bodies
catapult into children's open mouths

A woman with laugh lines
                      fat thumb
lifts
                      unlatches skin
torso in stunning cascade

Puckering waterfall
                      pubis thighs knee-folds
underneath

She is there
and gone

It is not important

the fundamental attitude of
All women

As two she moves in a distorted way
a woman loved by a man

Unmoored and generous with
her insides

Shared disaster throws light
on humanity's soft body

"What would I like to be?" You get the idea from a Canadian

A woman's wide eyes and a PIN for the joint account
instruments for survival in the glaring noise of day

In the produce aisle All eyes widen
a disembodied wail
                        cuts the sheets of hydration
the kale withers the apples brown

To lie so deeply she stretches the corners
of her mouths so wide as to swallow

Separate bodies return to losing
the unknown
                    if the heart
resides above

Its chamber the doll-like sweetheart will return
to life three times
                    if she is a crude lover
red and so vulnerable she is
a perfect container of incised skin

A larynx stands up in the body
hear the luscious echo

"There have been such a number of stunning attacks."
You were moved to say:

"She has about her a terrible aversion to leaving the house—"

She is searching for examples to parallel pot lids and dresses
to begin with as you recall she looked   a little drunk

Nipple spitting its nylon sutures   she moaned

You recall she returned to the mirror and asked
how it is one acts   in private

The burden of smiles sitting in the chest
a parachute

Sometimes now at night she thinks being alone
it's important

The receiver nowhere near her mouth

She a woman loved by a man became quiet
he carries on in real love

The action described above if correctly operating
will let you ask:

Her rosy snout is lifted to the future
what is it but a rectangle of light

The pleasant aroma of skin sack wafts
with a wanton impulse so like

A funny little girl

She hears the hush of all past mornings
narrow and vast

You could only think to fecundate yourself

What is want
little more than the wind

It is helpful to become more sensitive
jabbing dust motes on dead remote

These are the vague gestures of a green army
a nail hooks under a shell

                    Pulls away
the fragile casing

From the eyes of All women
                              you will feel

A woman longing

With wide hips they prefer to go deep within the body
feel the insertion point

"You might not have much to be worried about."

ORWOMEN

These eyes had   briefly excluded
                              the coffin-to-cradle remains

Awoman palms the right eyeball & strains short-sighted to see
beyond the jutt-

                    ing wall dividing dead legs
                              black stockings floral carpet

a picture of Jane

Down tumble   skid curl

                    wandered
beneath surface of
                    ring finger
& clotted blood

descended into waiting mouth
                              their roots
unsteady floorboards

Awoman likes it here
                    likes Jane better

Opened wide
                      wide enough to swallow

Wednesday afternoon

calculated movements from bed into kitchenette
and sitting room

                      Awoman
used to be
                      held

peach receiver   Cheryl's ribcage
                  pressing into her thighs
her ankles drinking

the low stone ceiling

She stayed on like shadows' fan blades
Aneye lash loosens itself from sheath

their being together
                    discarded like ash

mindful to forget
                    everything

                    a kiss
a hatbox

                                    her wits

Kay cross-legged in the kitchen hands behind her head
wrist deep in the damp pink tissue of

Awoman likes it here

the man & a mole on Kay's neck

There is a siren screaming a traffic accident a prowler
a homicide

& a high unexpected laugh from behind a closed door
into the ignored front hall into fretful sleep

They uncross Herlegs
button nose straight stare teeth tilling sharp words

still blood
                    stretched pale
what remains

an appointment for sex
is mistaken for the murmuring of animals

Jane keeps one houseplant
a rare plant

She purges her shoulders
mother's ravaged face Hercerebrum

wide pupils white front fruitful strikes
where Kay'd like a finger to be

It looks like she
tried

to call

for help

Orwomen squeal
tentatively through Cheryl's open kitchen

talking softly taking mouthfuls chalky pills

Spotted ring finger treads
below

hastening to draw body
up
                        pull
the outside in

Awoman opens her
                            mouth
for air

a body haunted mates in captivity a body no more

            Herthumb finds a squirming centipede

Someone believed in serial monogamy

Someone became headlines
neighbours used inside their countertops

In the dream there were too many colours for a clean wash
the quilt was ruined

Her family heirlooms
remind them
of you

Orwomen

In the dream the hands had been her own
turning solid keys in wavering air

a child's head whipped past blinked out

air
empty

child gone

in the dream she had been exactly herself
Awoman

the body within the mind

ACKNOWLEDGEMENTS

Thank you to Sarah Burgoyne, Paige Cooper, Jeff Noh, William Vallières, and Kasia van Schaik for reading. Thank you to Stephanie Bolster, Sina Queyras, and Gail Scott for teaching. Thank you to Andrew Faulkner and Leigh Nash for believing. Thank you to Jenny Sampirisi for seeing. Finally, thank you to Zac Abram for loving.

INVISIBLE PUBLISHING produces fine Canadian literature for those who enjoy such things. As an independent, not-for-profit publisher, our work includes building communities that sustain and encourage engaging, literary, and current writing.

Invisible Publishing has been in operation for over a decade. We released our first fiction titles in the spring of 2007, and our catalogue has come to include works of graphic fiction and non-fiction, pop culture biographies, experimental poetry, and prose.

We are committed to publishing diverse voices and experiences. In acknowledging historical and systemic barriers, and the limits of our existing catalogue, we strongly encourage writers from LGBTQ2SIA+ communities, Indigenous writers, and writers of colour to submit their work.

Invisible Publishing is also home to the Bibliophonic series of music books and the Throwback series of CanLit reissues.

If you'd like to know more, please get in touch:
info@invisiblepublishing.com

Invisible